I Belong to the Buddhist Faith

Katie Dicker and Nisansa De Silva

PowerKiDS
press

New York

Published in 2010 by The Rosen Publishing Group Inc.
29 East 21st Street, New York, NY 10010

First Edition

Library of Congress Cataloging-in-Publication Data

Dicker, Katie
  I belong to the Buddhist faith / Katie Dicker and Nisansa De Silva.
      p. cm. -- (I belong)
  Includes index.
  ISBN 978-1-4358-3031-8 (library binding)
  ISBN 978-1-4358-8616-2 (paperback)
  ISBN 978-1-4358-8617-9 (6-pack)
  1. Religious life--Buddhism--Juvenile literature. I. De Silva, Nisansa II. Title.
  BQ5395.D53 2010
  294.3--dc22
                            2008051875

Manufactured in China

Disclaimer

The text in this book is based on the experience of one family. Although every effort
has been made to offer accurate and clearly expressed information, the author and
publisher acknowledge that some explanations may not be relevant to those who
practice their faith in a different way.

Acknowledgements

The author and publisher would like to thank the following people for their help and
participation in this book:
The De Silva family, Samantha Palihakkara, Ven. Seelawimala, and Richard Jones.

Photography by Chris Fairclough.

Contents

Going to the vihara

Hi, I'm Nisansa. Today it's Saturday and I've come to the **vihara** with my mom and dad, and my brother, Sachith. We're Buddhists. We've come to give thanks for Lord Buddha's guidance.

We wear white clothes when we visit the vihara as a sign of peace. We've also brought flowers to offer to the Buddha.

LONDON BUDDHIST VIHARA

The vihara is open every day, but we usually go on the weekend. The vihara is the home of some Buddhist monks. It's a place for us to learn more about the Buddha's teachings and to see our Buddhist friends.

The monks wear traditional orange robes and shave their heads like the Buddha did long ago.

Who was the Buddha?

Lord Buddha was a prince named Siddhartha Gautama, who lived in India about 2,550 years ago. He had a comfortable life, but he realized sometimes people were unhappy. He wanted to find out how this unhappiness could be avoided.

This is a picture of Lord Buddha. He is sitting with his legs crossed because he's **meditating**.

Siddhartha Gautama left his palace and went on a long, difficult journey. One day, as he meditated under a bodhi tree, he realized that people can learn to be content with what they have, to avoid feelings of unhappiness. We call this understanding **Enlightenment**.

This bodhi tree at the vihara reminds me of the day Siddhartha Gautama saw the truth and became known as the Buddha—"the enlightened one."

The Buddha's teachings

The Buddha started teaching other people new ways of thinking, so they could achieve happiness. His teachings were later written down in an ancient language called Pali. These holy books are known as the **Tripitaka**.

The monks at the vihara can read Pali. They study the holy books and teach us what is written in them.

We all go to the **shrine** room to thank Lord Buddha for his guidance. As Buddhists, we think about the **Four Noble Truths**, and how we should behave in our lives to bring happiness to other people, too.

During a **service** at the vihara, the monks **chant** verses from the holy books. We join in with the chanting, wishing happiness to everyone.

Learning about the Buddha

I go to **Dhamma** school at the vihara. We read stories about Lord Buddha and his life. When Siddhartha Gautama left his palace, he lived in the forest before he gained Enlightenment.

Enlightenment is the complete understanding of our place in the world. I try to become enlightened by reading and following the Buddha's teachings.

The Buddha decided to live as a monk. He did not want to be worshipped as a god. Instead, his teachings are a guide to help people live a better, happier life.

Today, we're learning about how Lord Buddha taught us to be kind and honest, and to share things with other people.

Behaving like the Buddha

Buddhists believe that to find happiness we should care for other people. We should also feel comfortable with what we have and who we are. Lord Buddha said that living life in **moderation** would make us happier.

I thank Lord Buddha for guiding me in the way I think and act, and ask for his **blessings**.

We try to meditate like Lord Buddha. Meditation helps you to become calm and happy. When we meditate, we train our minds to concentrate only on good thoughts, and avoid thinking about bad things.

At home, I practice meditating with Mom. She teaches me to be still and to concentrate on my breathing.

Living a happy life

I try to follow the Buddha's teachings every day. Sometimes, I feel cross but then I remember bad feelings don't last forever. When I feel happy again, I think how right the Buddha is.

Sachith and I sometimes argue, but we laugh about it afterward. We try to bring happiness into the world by not speaking unkindly or harming anyone.

The Buddha showed us how important it is to look after each other. I try to be kind to other people and to show my family, friends, and teachers how much I care for them.

I try to help Mom at home. It's good to help other people, so they can have a better day.

Dana

There's a special service called **Dana** at the vihara every morning. People bring food for the monks. It makes me happy when I give and share what I have with others.

Each Dana ceremony has a different theme. Today, we're giving thanks for what our parents have done for us.

We offer our food to the Buddha first. We also bring flowers, light candles, and burn sweet incense. The shrine room is a very peaceful place to show our respect.

Candles remind me that the light of Lord Buddha's teachings will always help me to live a simple, peaceful, and happy life.

Food

Lord Buddha taught people to eat in moderation and to be happy with what they receive. For thousands of years, Buddhist monks have followed the Buddha's way of life and only have one or two meals a day.

It's noon and the monks are having their last meal today. They will just drink liquids in the afternoon and evening.

On special days, we have a celebration meal called "kiribath," which we eat with family and friends. Kiribath is a type of rice cooked in coconut milk—it tastes really good!

These traditional foods are from Sri Lanka where Mom and Dad were born. We often eat kiribath and sweet foods on festival days.

Buddhist festivals

Vesak Day is a celebration that reminds us of Lord Buddha's birth, enlightenment, and death. We believe all these important events happened in May, on the day of a full moon.

On Vesak Day, we clean our home and decorate the front of our house with lanterns. It gives us a happy, festive feeling.

Days of a full moon are special holy days for us. This is because many important events in **Buddhism** happened on the day of a full moon.

At New Year, we offer the monks these betel leaves. They also tie a piece of blessed string around our wrists to give us blessings for the year ahead.

Glossary, further information, and Web Sites

blessing to look after someone or something.

Buddhism the Buddhist religion.

chant to repeat words out loud, often in the same tone.

Dana the Pali word for giving and generosity.

Dhamma the Pali word for the Buddha's teachings.

Enlightenment to see things in their true light, as they really are.

Four Noble Truths the main teachings of the Buddha about overcoming unhappinness.

meditating sitting quietly and thinking about something very deeply.

moderation to avoid having too much or too little of something.

service a type of ceremony.

shrine a holy place where people pay their respect, often in front of a statue.

Tripitaka the holy books full of the Buddha's teachings.

vihara the home of Buddhist monks.

Did you know?

- Buddhism began in India about 2,550 years ago.
- There are around 350 million Buddhists today, mainly living in Asia.
- There are different types of Buddhists. These include Theravada Buddhists and Mahayana Buddhists.
- Most Buddhist festivals fall on the day of a full moon.

Activities

1. Make your own shrine. Draw a picture of the Buddha, and then find some flowers and candles to put around it.
2. Do you know any stories about the Buddha's life? Use books or the internet to find out some of these stories.
3. Write a poem about the Buddhist way of life.

Books to read

- *I Once was a Monkey: Stories Buddha Told*
  by Jeanne M. Lee (Farrar, Straus and Giroux, 1999)

- *This is my Faith: Buddhism*
  Anita Ganeri (Barron's Educational, 2006)

- *Traditional Religious Tales: Buddhist Stories*
  by Anita Ganeri (Picture Window Books, 2006)

Web Sites

Due to the changing nature of Internet links, PowerKids Press has developed an online list of Web sites related to the subject of this book. This site is updated regularly. Please use this link to access this list: www.powerkidslinks.com/blong/budd

Buddhist festivals

Buddhist New Year (Jan./Feb./Mar./Apr.) A time to think about how to live a better life. The Buddhist New Year falls in different months in different parts of the world.

Vesak Day (May/June) A festival to remember the birth, enlightenment, and death of the Buddha.

Dhamma Day (July) A festival to celebrate the Buddha's first teachings.

Sangha Day (November) A festival to celebrate friendship and to remember Buddhists around the world.

Buddhist symbols

Lotus flower a reminder of the Buddhist way of life. The Lotus flower grows in the mud at the bottom of a pool, but rises above the surface to become a beautiful flower.

Eight-spoked wheel the eight spokes are a symbol of the Buddha's teachings, called the Noble Eightfold Path (which forms the fourth Noble Truth). The wheel is a symbol of the cycle of life, death, and rebirth.

Index